100 IDEAS FOR EFFECTIVE SCHOOL ASSEMBLIES

DR DHEERAJ MEHROTRA

Copyright © Dr Dheeraj Mehrotra
All Rights Reserved.

ISBN 978-1-63850-961-5

This book has been published with all efforts taken to make the material error-free after the consent of the author. However, the author and the publisher do not assume and hereby disclaim any liability to any party for any loss, damage, or disruption caused by errors or omissions, whether such errors or omissions result from negligence, accident, or any other cause.

While every effort has been made to avoid any mistake or omission, this publication is being sold on the condition and understanding that neither the author nor the publishers or printers would be liable in any manner to any person by reason of any mistake or omission in this publication or for any action taken or omitted to be taken or advice rendered or accepted on the basis of this work. For any defect in printing or binding the publishers will be liable only to replace the defective copy by another copy of this work then available.

Contents

Preface	v
1. 100 Ideas For Effective School Assemblies	1
2. About The Author	39
3. Books By The Same Author	42
Source/ Reference/courtesy	45

Preface

The book, 100 Ideas For Effective School Assemblies, features a collection of ideas for assemblies ranging from thoughtful fact sharing moments to fun and information packed solutions to deliver a learning out come in the notion.

The book delivers a power packed solution to the concern towards making assemblies creative and informative.

*For comments and feedback send your inputs at **tqmhead@aol.com***

Best & Cheers!

www.authordheerajmehrotra.com

> "I like to listen. I have learned a great deal from listening carefully. Most people never listen."
> – Ernest Hemingway

I
100 Ideas For Effective School Assemblies

Picture Courtesy: Little Angels High School, Gwalior, India

The very importance of a school assembly lies towards the beginning of the day of learning on a positive note. The preface is towards starting the learning with the bright sun shine and the opportunity to the students to be a party to the learning. We do believe that Morning Assembly plays an important part in the holistic development of learners. It is a platform that provides young minds to boost their confidence towards public speaking and imbibing a feeling of team spirit.

The very purpose of the school assembly is to mark the beginning of the day, the preparedness for learning and experiencing the challenges and opportunities as it comes during the day. The morning assembly is the class of the Principal and is hence the most important part of the day's learning platform for the students and the teachers. It is the responsibility of the PRINCIPAL to assure and initiate the learning with creativity and deliberations during the assembly which largely lasts for around 35 to 40 minutes. The presentation during the assembly must be student oriented with learning as a priority. Normally, the routine activities in the morning assembly include prayer, hymns, thoughts, news, amazing facts, students talk (on famous personalities) and national anthem.

The following are some of the Ideas and Strategies which can be adopted to make the presentations and deliberations effective and strong.

#1

An Assembly is the Class of the PRINCIPAL of the school. Hence it is essential for him/ her to be present every day without fail.

#2

Make sure your assembly uses suitable language and ideas for your audience, and that the extra resources you decide to include are suitable for the age group who will experience it.

#3

It is important therefore, that when the children come together for a school assembly, they know that it is something more special than their normal learning module.

#4

Children enter and leave the hall quietly, but should also be given a time to reflect while in the hall. Hence, prayers can also follow and be followed by a few moments of silence. This can be very effective, especially if the children are not expecting it.

#5

Think about the way you deliver your assembly, what tools you will use to ensure it captures the attention of the specific age group, and that it is accessible to pupils of all abilities and creative minds.

Picture Courtesy: Little Angels High School (LAHS), Gwalior, India

#6

A successful assembly is one that manages to inspire the audience and get the message across in an engaging manner.

#7

Your presentation is key to delivering a successful assembly.

#8

Make sure everyone is able to see and hear you as well as any extra resources you are using.

#9

When the whole school is assembled, this seems a good time to give out notices and to remind the children about behaviour and a repeat of rules/ regulations.

#10

Think about the ways you can make your assembly memorable. This could be through choice of song, music, participation or visual stimulus (you could use ICT whiteboards).

Picture Courtesy: Little Angels High School (LAHS), Gwalior, India

#11

You could invite someone into school to talk to pupils.

#12

Where possible, link the assembly to the relevant curriculum areas. Think about which topics the assembly will support. It is likely that there will be key academic links and additions could be social, moral, cultural and spiritual links.

#13

The better prepared you are, the more successful the assembly is likely to be. Will pupils participate in the assembly? If so, do the pupils need to be prepared? Or is participation intended to be spontaneous? Could you invite other teachers or members of the community in to talk to pupils about their relevant experiences? Think about the logistics of your audience.

#14

If you are explaining complex moral issues, think about your audience and the best way to deliver your assembly. If your audience includes a wide variety of ages and abilities, always make sure everyone will understand, including the youngest in the group.

#15

Music and songs can create a great atmosphere, and can very often aid understanding.

Picture Courtesy: Little Angels High School (LAHS), Gwalior, India

#16

It is important to remember the pupils are heading straight back to class after your assembly. Choose your music carefully: if they get too fired up you may be unpopular with your colleagues!

#17

Assure Attendance of All

Children like to see their teachers and helpers present in school assemblies.

#18

Have success sharing:

Achievement Assemblies to celebrate successes of individual pupils, such as: examination success, acquisition of new skills, helping others, bravery etc.

#19

Explore Merit Assemblies:

Once a week, maybe during the House assembly, a merit badge can be presented to one child from each class. These can be awarded for academic success, effort, good progress, social skills etc.

#20

Common prayer:

Our Father who art in heaven, hallowed be thy name. Thy kingdom come, thy will be done, on earth as it is in heaven. Give us this day our daily bread and forgive us our trepasses, as we forgive those who trespass against us. And lead us not into temptation, but deliver us from evil.

Picture Courtesy: Little Angels High School (LAHS), Gwalior

#21

Have a Teacher's Talk

Probably the class teacher of the class presenting the assembly.

#22

Must be addressed at least once a week by the PRINCIPAL

But the Principal must attend it daily and show her presence as an observer.

#23

Have a NATIONAL ANTHEM and PLEDGE Daily.

#24

Share no negative NEWS....

Be positive and polished in sharing the news.

#25

Celebrate occasions and important days in the assembly but within the time frame.

Picture Courtesy: Little Angels High School (LAHS), Gwalior, India

#26

Sing a song

Music make the living go LIVE !

#27

Motivate and empower the class who conducts the assembly best by honouring them with certificates of merit and sweets.

#28

Have a Birthday Song for all who have a Birthday by calling them on the screen ONCE a week. Including the teachers if any.

#29

Invite visitors to speak on and bless the children from time to time. This can be the TOP Management to the DOOR man! Learning counts.

#30

Explore the world by REGULAR NEWS/ DISCUSSIONS/ QUIZZES

Honour Students who answer the Quiz well.

#31

Honour the class and the students who present the Assembly well.

#32

Pre- inform the school which class is going to conduct the Assembly the Next working day.

#33

Use Digital Games and recognise the participants with the best online revert. Mention the achievers of the best blogging and social media share.

#34

Have a Book Review. Let the students celebrate the review as a deliberations and honour them before the masses.

#35

Organise Inter Class Competitions on Reading. The students may be given random text to read.

Select the students too randomly.

#35

Practice Yoga as a regular event.

#37

Organise the whole Assembly in some foreign Language/ Local Language.

#38

Celebrate the Festival During an Assembly.

#39

Sing a Song of Fellowship and World Peace.

#40

Have Animal Awareness as theme of the assembly.

Picture Courtesy: Little Angels High School (LAHS), Gwalior, India

#41

Celebrate the National Day of various countries

#42

Talk about Currencies of various nations as a theme

#43

Invite Parents as Guest Speakers on random basis

#44

Have a Quality Circle Presentation

#45

Organise World Peace Prayer as an activity

#46

Add a stimulus. A video clip is a great way to get your message across and engage children

#47

Remember that announcements should not take over and eat into the time planned for the assembly itself.

#48

Assure no wastage of time. An assembly works best if it starts before or as the pupils enter the room.

#49

Before Your let your children speak. Think is it really True, Helpful, Inspiring, Necessary and Kind.

#50

Share Teacher's Talk Crisp and Short with some lesson as a story telling.

Picture Courtesy: Little Angels High School (LAHS), Gwalior, India

#51

Teach Value of Education not Value Education through deliberations and role plays.

#52

Teach 360 degree framework through universal values and peace education.

#53

Teachers should deliver a value based talk every day on rotation.

#54

A day may be reserved for a General Knowledge discussion in the class rooms on topics of current - national and international issues in addition to a 5 minute introduction during the assembly to gather preparedness of the participation of the students.

#55

Classes should be honoured for 100% Attendance for one week on MONDAYS. This creates a great motiation for the students to attend classes regularly.

#56

Have Fashion Shows related to various Career Options with showcase of challenges and opportunities for each profession displayed.

#57

Honour the parents of the Students Randomly for the Best Groomed/ Best Disciplined Children on one of the days of the week.

#58

Award the Best House Assembly and Best Class Assembly boards to the outstanding presentations.

#59

Use the following themes for the Assembly:

- My School
- Discipline
- Time Management
- Patience And Perseverance
- Self-Discipline Is The Best Discipline
- Failure To Success

- A Goal Without A Plan Is Just A Wish
- Health Is Wealth
- Unity In Diversity
- Our National Heroes
- Good Manners And Good Etiquette
- Our Environment
- Teachers- Ladders Of Society
- Character And Success
- Child's Safety
- The Importance Of Perseverance To Achieve Goals
- A Good Leader
- Determination
- Being A Good Citizen
- Aspiration
- Discoveries And Inventions
- Wonders Of Science
- Safer Internet
- Caring For Our Wildlife
- Our Place In The Society
- Caring For Others
- New Resolutions
- Abilities And Achievement
- Be A Hero
- Being Different
- Great Scientists
- Forgiveness
- Design Thinking
- Creativity
- Life Skills
- Experiential Learning

#60

Have a model class presentation once a month.

Picture Courtesy: Little Angels High School (LAHS), Gwalior, India

#61

Depict an episode of MUN (Model United Nations) once a month to enrich about the event and its benefits.

#62

Showcase rules and regulations of at least one SPORT once a month as a presentation.

#63

Showcase about the causes and remedies of at least one DISEASE once a month as a presentation.

#64

Have a presentation of any country's flag.

#65

Organise an event based on house wise deliberation on Budget which may include State Budget and the Central Budget

#66

Organise a Talk Show with some Invited GUEST once a month.

#67

Play some TED Talk video (Maximum 5 minutes) using the Audio/ Video Setup.

#68

Organise an event on importance of Truthfulness via a road show on

"Truthfulness is the foundation of all Human Virtues."

#69

Hold Story Telling Activity once a month. The main objective of this activity is to develop students' communication skills and expanding the realm of their imagination.

#70

Organise events to raise awareness of the vast and diverse cultural heritage of our country and promote creative thinking in the students. This can be done via activities like making Travel Brochure, Showcasing various crops and festivals of the state as an inter house event.

Picture Courtesy: Little Angels High School (LAHS), Gwalior, India

#71

Organise SDG events like decoration of dustbins from easy available materials like cardboard, waste plastic etc and raised awareness regarding different types of waste and it's

segregation.

#72

Invite Local Bodies like Police/ Medical/ Cleanliness/ Municipal representatives for a Talk on public policies.

#73

Invite Bank Officials/ Hospital Heads/ CEOs for TALK on respective professions to motivate the students.

#74

Organise Story Telling Competition Class wise with Grand Parents as Judges.

#75

Organise an event as a regular learning on building a better vocabulary through surprise quizzes and deliberations.

#76

Promote linguistic, cultural diversity and multilingualism through Language Day Celebration at least once a month during the assembly.

#77

Promote curated weekly news capsule specially designed for children of all age groups. The news can be filtered and should be aimed at making children familiar with general knowledge to be future-ready.

#78

Make sure all your assemblies are covered by social media handles including YouTube, Twitter and Facebook of the school on a regular basis.

#79

Organise Passion School with Parents. Here the learners may swap roles with teachers and parents can become learners resulting in a grand success.

#80

Events like celebrating International Mountain day help students to learn to become individuals, who understand their responsibilities towards preserving Earth's natural resources and saving environment by contributing to their barest minimum.

Picture Courtesy: Little Angels High School (LAHS), Gwalior, India

#81

Organise WORK EDUCATION SESSIONS by inviting parents to share their professional standards and commitments to the society at large.

#82

Orgainse Parent Participation Programmes to deliver extraordinary innovations in the world and the ideas that led to those innovations. This would prove to be an enriching session and befitting to the inquisitive and curious young minds.

#83

Teach Life Skills as a habit through role models, nukkar natak, showcasing and class presentations frequently.

#84

Organise short Language Orientation Sessions with an inception towards instilling an approbation for multilingualism at a young age.

#85

Organise LIVE sharing Assemblies via WEBINARS with various other schools PAN India to enrich learning and understanding the cultural heritage.

#86

Celebrate birthdays as Kindness Days and let the children be familiar with the positive effects of good deeds and that the kindness is the common thread that unites us all.

#87

Host business case studies by senior children as an endeavour to foster entrepreneurial culture and ethical leadership among the students.

#88

Initiate the mental health movement via "Enforcing Positive Mental Health", "The Power of Optimism", "Gender Sensitivity" and "Turning Challenges into Opportunities". These may be conducted as an event by the houses and would be a great learning opportunity for the students.

#89

Organise Ramp Walk flagging Peace and Prosperity through slogans class wise. This can be once in a month event through proper planning and execution.

#90

Conduct interactive sessions of Learning to express emotions in a positive way through Teacher Talks. This further helps children to develop the skills to regulate emotions well and leads to positive attitudes and behaviours later in life.

#91

Celebrate days of PEACE and FESTIVITY through World Peace Prayer Ceremonies, this helps to strengthen and embolden the principles of peace, both within and among all nations and people. Let students be the harbingers of Peace via role plays and deliberations.

#92

Encourage poets in making by organising Hindi/ English self composed poems. This shall encourage students towards presenting a musical rendition of self composed poems welcoming Spring - the king of seasons as an example.

#93

Deliver happiness quotient through JOKE time, singing, dancing and sharing life stories at least once a month.

#94

Discuss AUTHOR of the week and share some of his/ her books.

#95

Play CROSSWORD as a fun activity by distributing photo copy. This can be an event once a month and declare winners who deliver the answers in shortest time.

#96

Organise Young Ideators Event, house wise with the best IDEA to save the ENVIRONMENT towards attaining the Sustainable Development Goals as a priority.

#97

Celebrate achievements of ALUMNI by inviting them in the school assembly and honour them.

#98

Conduct Alumni Knowledge Sharing event once a month towards counselling and career advice for the students.

#99

Observe the Nutrition Day and take the #EatHealthy challenge. Encourage students to make only healthy food choices. This would Give their body the power of nutritious food. Arrange "Do it yourself" events of preparing dry kitchen meals and let the students encourage people around them to choose a healthier lifestyle leading to a balanced body, mind and soul.

#100

Let the Students Council interact with the students and listen to their problems at least once a month. This can be an open forum guided and facilitated by the teachers.

II
About the Author

Dheeraj Mehrotra, MS, MPhil, Ph.D. (Education Management) honoris causa., a white and a yellow belt in SIX SIGMA, a Certified NLP Business Diploma holder, is an Educational Innovator, Author, with expertise in Six Sigma In Education, Academic Audits, Neuro Linguistic Programming (NLP), Total Quality Management In Education, an Experiential Educator, a CBSE Resource towards School Assessment (SQAA), CCE, JIT, Five S and KAIZEN. He has authored over 40 books on Computer Science for ICSE/ ISC/ CBSE Students, over 10 books of academic interest for the field of education excellence and Six Sigma. A former Principal at De Indian Public School, New Delhi, (INDIA) with an ample teaching experience of over Two Decades, he is a certified Trainer for Quality Circles/ TQM in Education and QCI Standards for School Accreditation/ Six Sigma in Education. He has also been honored with the President of India's National Teacher Award in the year 2006 and the Best Science Teacher State Award (By the Ministry of Science and Technology, State of UP), Innovation in Education for his inception of Six

Sigma In Education by Education Watch, New Delhi and Education World- Best Teacher Award, BOLT Learner Teacher Award by Air India, 'Innovation in Education Award 2016' by Higher Education Forum (HEF), Gujarat Chapter, among others. He has developed over 150 FREE EDUCATIONAL MOBILE Apps for the Google Play Store exclusively for Teachers, Students and Parents. This work has been recognized by the LIMCA BOOK OF RECORDS & INDIA BOOK OF RECORDS as the only Indian to draw that feast. Dr. Mehrotra is presently working as an Academic Evangelist in India. He has conducted over 1000 workshops globally on "Excellence In Education" integrated with Total Quality Management and Six Sigma, Technology Integration in Education (TIE), Developing towards being ROCKSTAR TEACHERS, including Cyberspace, Cyber Security, Classroom Management, School Leadership & Management and Innovative teaching within classrooms via Mind Maps, NLP and Experiential Learning in Academics. He is an active TEDx speaker and can be viewed at youtube tedX channel. He has developed over 350 UDEMY Courses and can be reached on www.authordheerajmehrotra.com

DR DHEERAJ MEHROTRA

www.authordheerajmehrotra.com

III
Books By The Same Author

100 IDEAS FOR EFFECTIVE SCHOOL ASSEMBLIES

Available at Amazon!

Source/ Reference/Courtesy

Picture Courtesy: Little Angels High School (LAHS), Gwalior, India

www.authordheerajmehrotra.com

https://www.amazon.in/Books-Dheeraj-Mehrotra/ s?rh=n%3A976389031%2Cp_27%3ADheeraj+Mehrotra

www.ingramcontent.com/pod-product-compliance
Lightning Source LLC
LaVergne TN
LVHW021740060526
838200LV00052B/3379